A RAIN FOREST Food Chain

A WHO-EATS-WHAT Adventure in South America

Rebecca Hogue Wojahn   Donald Wojahn

Lerner Publications Company
Minneapolis

For Eli and Cal. We hope this answers some of your questions.

There are many links in the chain that created this series. Thanks to Ann Kerns, Carol Hinz, Danielle Carnito, Sarah Olmanson, Paul Rodeen, the staff of the L. E. Phillips Memorial Library, and finally, Katherine Hogue

Lerner Publications Company
A division of Lerner Publishing Group, Inc.
241 First Avenue North
Minneapolis, MN 55401 U.S.A.

Website address: www.lernerbooks.com

Library of Congress Cataloging-in-Publication Data

Wojahn, Rebecca Hogue.
    A rain forest food chain : A who-eats-what adventure in South America / by Rebecca Hogue Wojahn and Donald Wojahn.
       p.   cm. — (Follow that food chain)
    Includes bibliographical references and index.
    ISBN 978-0-8225-7497-2 (lib. bdg. : alk. paper)
    1. Rain forest ecology—South America—Juvenile literature. 2. Food chains (Ecology) —South America—Juvenile literature. I. Title.
QH111.W65 2009
577.34098—dc22   2008021112

Manufactured in the United States of America
1 2 3 4 5 6 – BP – 14 13 12 11 10 09

Contents

Introduction

Hot, wet air wraps around you as you step into the **rain forest**. Thick, green leaves and vines tangle everywhere. High above in the treetop, hoots, screeches, and tweets echo from creatures you can't see. Then the rain starts again.

Rain forests get more rainfall than any other place on Earth. That's what makes the plants grow like crazy here. In fact, the trees and vines are so thick that it takes ten minutes for the rain to drip down to you on the ground. Plants aren't the only living things that thrive in the rain forest, though. More than half of all the world's animals live in rain forests. Scientists discover new **species** of animals, birds, and insects hidden in the jungle every day.

This rain forest is in South America. It spreads out from the world's widest river, the Amazon. The Amazon rain forest is a tropical rain forest. The weather is hot and rainy all year long.

Nearly one-third of South America is a rain forest. But despite its size, this rain forest is in danger. Every minute, the South American rain forest shrinks. By the time you finish reading this page, a space the size of your school playground will have been cleared for farming or building. With it go the **habitats** of thousands of species of unique animals. Come meet a few of them in this book.

Venezuela
Guyana
Suriname
French Guiana
Colombia
Ecuador
SOUTH AMERICA
Peru
Bolivia
Brazil
Pacific Ocean
Chile
Paraguay
Atlantic Ocean
Argentina
Uruguay

N

MILES
0   200   400   600
0   200 400 600 800
KM.

■ Amazon rain forest

5

The New World

North America, Central America, and South America are sometimes called the New World. Some plants and animals from these regions are described as New World. You may hear or read about New World monkeys, New World felines (cats), or New World crops. That term helps people tell those plants and animals apart from plants and animals from Africa, Asia, or Europe.

Choose a
TERTIARY CONSUMER

All the living things in the rain forest are necessary for its health and survival. From the anaconda twisting through the water, to ants swarming over the leaves on the ground, all living things are connected. Animals and other organisms feed on and transfer energy to one another. This is called a **food chain** or a **food web**.

In food chains, the strongest **predators** are called **tertiary consumers**. They hunt other animals for food and have few natural enemies. Some of the animals they eat are called **secondary consumers**. Secondary consumers are also predators. They hunt plant-eating animals. Plant eaters are **primary consumers**.

Plants are **producers**. Using energy from the sun, they produce their own food. Plants take in **nutrients** from the soil. They also provide nutrients to the animals that eat them.

Decomposers are insects or **bacteria** that break down dead plants and animals. Decomposers change them into the nutrients found in the soil.

The plants and animals in a food chain depend on one another. Sometimes there's a break in the chain, such as one type of animal dying out. This loss ripples through the rest of the habitat.

Begin your journey through the rain forest food web by choosing a powerful **carnivore**, or meat eater. These tertiary consumers are at the top of the food chain. That means that, for the most part, they don't have any enemies in the rain forest (except for humans).

When it's time for the tertiary consumer to eat, pick its meal and flip to that page. As you go through the book, don't be surprised if you backtrack and end up where you never expected to be. That's how food webs work—they're complicated. And watch out for those dead ends! When you hit one of those, you have to go back to page 7 and start over with another tertiary consumer.

The main role an animal plays in the rain forest food web is identified by a color-coded shape. Here is the key to that code:

TERTIARY CONSUMER

PRODUCER

SECONDARY CONSUMER

PRIMARY CONSUMER

DECOMPOSER

7

To choose . . .

. . . a jaguar, TURN TO PAGE 8.
. . . an anaconda, TURN TO PAGE 26.
. . . a harpy eagle, TURN TO PAGE 37.

To learn more about the rain forest food web, TURN TO PAGE 47.

JAGUAR *(Panthera onca)*

The jaguar pads through the forest. Outside the jungle, this big cat's brilliant spotted coat would stand out. But in the rain forest, the coat helps hide the jaguar. His dark and light spots blend right in to the leafy shadows around him.

The jaguar is large—as big as an adult man. He crouches. He's spotted a favorite meal grazing ahead. It's a peccary—a small pig-like animal.

Native South Americans call the jaguar *yaguara*. That means "the animal that kills in a single bound." But he only kills so easily if he's lucky. Unlike other large cats, such as cheetahs, jaguars aren't speedy. They need to surprise their **prey** and snap its spine immediately. Otherwise, it escapes—like now. The jaguar pounces, but the peccary squeals and shoots off into the jungle. The strongest predator in the New World and the world's third-largest cat has just missed his mark. He growls in complaint.

Not that long ago, jaguars were hunted for their beautiful coats. Killing a jaguar is no longer legal. But "green" hunting is being experimented with. Green hunting is when people pay to track a jaguar and then shoot it with a tranquilizer (a drug that makes the animal sleep). While the jaguar is asleep, green hunters put a radio collar around its neck. The collar sends out radio signals that scientists can follow on their equipment. This allows scientists to track where jaguars go. By tracking the jaguar, we can learn more about its habits.

Because jaguars are rare, roam so far, and hunt at night, they are hard to find and study. Scientists have used unusual methods to try to learn more about them. Researchers set up "camera traps" for jaguars. These cameras are placed in the jungle. They are heat sensitive. They will only snap pictures if something warm, such as a living animal, is in front of the camera lens. Of course, the warm body isn't always a jaguar, so scientists catch all sorts of animals on film.

The night grows darker as the jaguar brushes past the thick tangle of leaves. He has a range of more than 100 square miles (260 square kilometers) in which he prowls for food. That sounds like a big territory. But jaguars are slowly getting squeezed out of space they need to survive. They have less than half the space they had one hundred years ago. And the big prey they prefer, such as peccaries and tapirs, are disappearing quickly too.

The jaguar heads down to a nearby stream. Without hesitation, he plunges into the water. He's a strong swimmer, and he hopes to find fish to catch tonight. Instead, he spies an agouti getting a drink. In a flash, he's snagged the rodent.

He drags the carcass out of the water and up the riverbank. He'll find a quiet spot to eat where his meal is less likely to be stolen by another predator. He gorges himself until his stomach swells. Now, it's off to find his den.

Hunting has gone well lately. *Last night for dinner, the jaguar pounced on...*

... a capybara grazing near the shore of a river. To find out what another capybara is up to, TURN TO PAGE 12.

... a giant armadillo, rolled up in a ball. To find out what another giant armadillo is up to, TURN TO PAGE 29.

... a green iguana that thought it was hidden from view. To find out what another green iguana is up to, TURN TO PAGE 18.

... a black howler monkey screeching out a warning. To find out what another black howler monkey is up to, TURN TO PAGE 34.

... a two-toed sloth hanging from a branch. To find out what another two-toed sloth is up to, TURN TO PAGE 14.

... a golden lion tamarin grooming himself. To find out what another golden lion tamarin is up to, TURN TO PAGE 46.

... a giant anteater snuffling in the dirt. To find out what another giant anteater is up to, TURN TO PAGE 22.

CAPYBARA (Hydrochaeris hydrochaeris)

A lone capybara snuffles through the grass near a pond. He's a rodent—related to rats and chipmunks. In fact, he looks like a supersized, tail-less squirrel. At 4 feet (1.2 meters) long and more than 100 pounds (45 kilograms), he's bigger than most fourth graders.

He stops at the trunk of a tree. At the top of his large snout is a scent gland. He rubs it on the leaves and tree trunk, leaving a scent marking.

Close by is a group of capybaras. But the lone capybara is a stranger to them. The group's leader thinks the lone capybara doesn't belong. The leader pushes through the other capybaras and trots over. He charges, and the two push each other before the newcomer backs down. The leader goes back to the center of the group where he gets the most protection and the best food. The newcomer stays at the edge of the group.

Suddenly, the capybaras on the other side of the group bark. A jaguar is coming! The capybara hurries into the nearby pond. There he hides out in the weeds along the shore. Only his eyes, ears, and nose are above water. Capybaras are right at home in the water. They have webbed feet for swimming and can hold their breath underwater.

When the jaguar moves on, the capybara steps out of the water and begins munching. Capybaras are very picky eaters and only eat a few types of plants. Their grazing also actually encourages growth in the plants they eat.

Last night for dinner, the capybara ate...

. . . leaves from a bromeliad.
To find out what the bromeliads of the rain forest are like, TURN TO PAGE 24.

. . . leaves from a kapok tree.
To find out what the trees of the rain forest are like, TURN TO PAGE 43.

. . . leaves from a vine. To find out what the lianas, vines, and creepers of the rain forest are like, TURN TO PAGE 50.

TWO-TOED SLOTH
(Choloepus didactylus)

The sloth hangs. And sleeps. And waits. Slowly, he turns his head and stretches out to a new branch. He pulls it closer and then strips its leaves off with his tongue. Now it's time for more hanging. And sleeping. And waiting.

Why are sloths so slow? Their bodies have adapted (changed over time) to match their leafy diet. Most animals that eat only plants have to graze all the time. They have to eat large amounts of grass and leaves to get the energy they need. Sloths don't need to eat much food. But in exchange, they have less energy to move around. Their body temperature is low. That helps them conserve, or save, energy. They also save energy by hardly moving.

This sloth has hung upside down on this branch for days. He spends so much time upside down that the hair on his body grows backward—from his belly to his back. His long claws make hanging perfectly easy and comfortable. Sloths have such a good grip that if they die while hanging, they may still cling to the tree for days.

This sloth rarely travels to the forest floor. Why should he? His food is up here. He can find water in the leaves too. He only comes down to relieve himself—and he can hold his urine and poop for a week!

It's a good thing he doesn't have to travel much. He can't walk on his back legs. They are too weak. He has to drag himself with his front legs, and that makes him even slower.

Last night for dinner, the sloth nibbled . . .

Green Fur

Sloths are almost a whole habitat themselves. They don't start out life with that greenish fur. That's algae (tiny living creatures) growing in their hair. The color of the algae helps sloths blend in with their surroundings. When sloths are still (which is most of the time), it's almost impossible to spot them in the trees. Sometimes, sloths will even take a few licks at their fur for a quick snack of algae. And algae aren't the only thing growing in that fur. Moths live there too. It's a perfect habitat for the insects—safe from birds, with lots of algae to eat.

... brazil nut leaves. To find out what the trees of the rain forest are like, TURN TO PAGE 43.

... leaves from a bromeliad. To find out what the bromeliads of the rain forest are like, TURN TO PAGE 24.

... liana leaves. To find out what the lianas, vines, and creepers of the rain forest are like, TURN TO PAGE 50.

ANTBIRDS *(Thamnophilidae)*

Watch out! A flock of forty tiny birds swoops overhead. They dazzle in their variety—there are more than twenty different kinds. Most birds only hang out with their own species. But antbirds will fly in mixed flocks. This makes it even harder for researchers to learn about these rain forest creatures.

In fact, scientists are discovering new antbird species all the time. So far, scientists have listed more than two hundred different kinds of antbirds. Many live only in certain regions of the rain forest or near certain types of plants.

Some antbirds follow swarms of army ants through the jungle. But they don't eat the ants. They let the ants scare up katydids, crickets, beetles, spiders, and scorpions out from under the dead leaves. Then the antbirds take their pick as if they're at a buffet. They've even come up with a way to balance on a vertical stick. From that perch, they can eat the insects but not get caught up in the ant swarm. Ant swarms will devour anything they come across, and the antbirds don't want to become an ant meal.

Last night for dinner, these antbirds snapped up...

Nervous Birds?

Bicolored antbirds twitch constantly. They slide their feet up and down the branch they are perched on. They fluff their tail feathers. Then they start all over again. At first, this behavior seems like a nervous habit. But the behavior actually helps the antbirds. The feet-sliding knocks any ants off their perch. So does the tail fluffing. The antbirds don't want to get surrounded by hungry ants.

... a young pink-toed tarantula, crouched, waiting for prey. To find out what another pink-toed tarantula is up to, TURN TO PAGE 20.

... a rhinoceros beetle rooting in the dead leaves. To find out what another rhinoceros beetle is up to, TURN TO PAGE 52.

GREEN IGUANA *(Iguana iguana)*

Flick. Flick. Flick. The iguana's tongue slides in and out of his mouth as he basks in the sun on a branch of a kapok tree. As a snake does, the iguana gathers smells in the air on his tongue. His tongue brings the smells to his Jacobson's organ. This organ at the top of his mouth is connected to the iguana's brain. It tells him what's near— food, water, or danger.

He grips the branch with his long claws and balances himself with a tail longer than his body. That long tail comes in handy when he's threatened. The iguana will swing and snap it just like a whip.

The Jacobson's organ isn't the only unusual part of the iguana's head. The iguana has a third eye too. We can't see it from the outside, but it's there at the top of his head, under his skin. Scientists think it helps the iguana sense light and dark. That's especially important to the iguana. He needs to soak up the warm sun, or he'll get too cold and die. He spends most of his days in the trees. He comes down to the forest floor only for food and mating.

Last night for dinner, he chomped . . .

Threats to Iguanas

As with many animals, a green iguana's biggest danger comes from people. When people cut down rain forest trees and plants, the iguanas' habitat is lost. People also capture many iguanas for food. In fact, iguanas are sometimes called *gallina de palo*—"chicken of the tree." And people catch iguanas and ship them off to be sold in pet stores. Many iguanas don't survive. If you are interested in having an iguana or other rain forest animal as a pet, you should check to be sure that it wasn't captured and stolen from the wild.

. . . a hoatzin pecking at a piece of fruit. To find out what another hoatzin is up to, TURN TO PAGE 56.

. . . a termite or two as they passed by. To find out what other termites are up to, TURN TO PAGE 42.

. . . leaves from a liana. To find out what the lianas, vines, and creepers of the rain forest are like, TURN TO PAGE 50.

. . . a rhinoceros beetle. Crunchy! To find out what another rhinoceros beetle is up to, TURN TO PAGE 52.

PINK-TOED TARANTULA *(Avicularia avicularia)*

The young tarantula lurks under the edge of the stone. He hunts by night. He has eight eyes, but they're tiny and don't see very well. But he doesn't need them. Each of his eight bristly legs has a pad of sticky hair. The hairs sense vibrations, which help the tarantula get around in the dark.

He's not looking for **prey** right now. He's in the midst of something else. His heart pounds. He flips onto his back. Suddenly, a crack opens in his exoskeleton—his hard outer shell. It slits wider as he wiggles. Slowly, he pulls his pink-tipped toes one at a time from his old shell.

He's molting, or getting a new "skin" from the inside out. But it's not just a fresh exterior. Molting replaces the lining of his stomach, his lungs and, if he's been injured, any missing legs! Male tarantulas only molt until they're full grown, but females molt throughout their lives.

After he emerges in his new skin, he'll rest for a few days. It takes that long for his exoskeleton to harden up. *Good thing he dined just a few days ago on . . .*

Poisonous Hunters

When a tarantula first attacks, it sinks its fangs into its victim. The fangs contain venom, or poison. The poison paralyses the tarantula's prey. The tarantula holds its dinner down with short minilegs called pedipalps and squirts juice from its stomach into its prey. The strong chemicals turn the prey's insides into jelly. Then—slurp! The tarantula sucks it down, leaving the outer husk of the animal behind. Tarantulas are dangerous hunters for many rain forest creatures. But they're not usually harmful to humans.

20

. . . an antbird cleaning up after a swarm of army ants. To find out what another antbird is up to, TURN TO PAGE 16.

. . . a giant monkey frog, resting on a leaf. To find out what another giant monkey frog is up to, TURN TO PAGE 54.

. . . a young green iguana, hiding under a branch for the night. To find out what another green iguana is up to, TURN TO PAGE 18.

. . . a hoatzin chick that had tumbled out of its nest. To find out what another hoatzin is up to, TURN TO PAGE 56.

. . . a swallow-tailed hummingbird, snatched from midair near a flower. To find out what another swallow-tailed hummingbird is up to, TURN TO PAGE 40.

. . . a rhinoceros beetle scuttling through the leaves. To find out what another rhinoceros beetle is up to, TURN TO PAGE 52.

GIANT ANTEATER *(Myrmecophaga tridactyla)*

The giant anteater slashes at the earth, digging a hole with her 6-inch (15-centimeter) claws. Ah, here's what she's been hoping for. She sticks her long snout into the hole and licks up the ants she's uncovered.

She is designed just for this task. Her mouth is long and narrow—only as wide as your pinky finger. From it extends an amazing tongue. The tongue is about 22 inches (56 cm) long. As speedy as it is long, the tongue can lap over 150 times a minute. The anteater snags hundreds of ants with the tongue's sticky surface. Anteaters are toothless, so she crushes the ants against the bony top of her mouth. Then she swallows. Sand and stones in her stomach help her further grind the ants up and digest them.

As good as the meal is here, she's not greedy at this nest. She eats for a few minutes and then moves on. If she lingered, the ants would have time to start biting back!

The anteater doesn't have a permanent home. Her time is spent wandering and eating. At 85 pounds (39 kilograms)—about the size of a large dog—she needs a lot of ants. She eats up to thirty thousand each day to survive. Good thing there can be more than fifty different species of ants on a single tree in the rain forest.

Last night for dinner, the giant anteater ate...

Big Claws

claws, so perfect for scraping
...und, are great weapons
...attacked by a predator,
...eater rises up on its rear
...lashes out. They try to hug
...cker and sink their claws in.
...have to be careful, or they can
...the one that ends up dead! In
...nt anteaters' claws are so long
...animals walk on the sides of
...ws. That way, they don't snag
...ws on sticks and roots.

... **army ants marching across the forest floor.** To find out what other army ants are up to, TURN TO PAGE 68.

Please return the items by the
due date(s) listed below, to
any Memphis Public Library
location.   For renewals:
Automated line: 452-2047
Cherokee Branch: 415-2762
Online: www.memphislibrary.org

Date due: 10/11/2014,23:59
Item ID: 0115272399151
Title: Ecosystems
Author: Richardson, Gillian.

Date due: 10/11/2014,23:59
Item ID: 0115240226387
Title: Forest fare : studying food webs in
  the forest
Author: Lundgren, Julie K.

Date due: 10/11/2014,23:59
Item ID: 0115243488919
Title: Life in a rain forest
Author: Levine, Stuart P., 1968-

Date due: 10/11/2014,23:59
Item ID: 0115272946001
Title: A rain forest food chain : A who-ea
ts-what advent
Author: Wojahn, Rebecca Hogue.

NO RENEWALS FOR:
Audio-visual material or
7-day Popular Library books
****
In the interest of providing
our customers with the best
library experience possible,
please take a few minutes to
complete a brief, confidential
survey, which can be accessed
at:
http://tinyurl.com/mplsurvey
Thank you!

BROMELIADS *(Bromeliaceae)*

The tight, overlapping leaves of this bromeliad flower houses its own world. Within its leaves, snails snack, insects hide, frogs lay eggs, and lizards doze. Bromeliads can grow on the ground. But in the rain forest, most are found growing on trees.

Plants such as bromeliads that grow against or on other plants are called **epiphytes**. But bromeliads don't draw food from the trees. They use the tree only for support. Their stiff, waxy leaves collect water and nutrients all on their own. If you look closely, the leaves are covered with special hairs that absorb the nutrients and water.

Two bromeliads grow on this tree branch.

Most bromeliads sprout huge, colorful flowers. The flowers attract birds, bats, and insects. Each visit from an outsider helps the bromeliad to **pollinate**. But bromeliads only have one bloom in them. After the flower has died, the bromeliad sends out a new shoot called a "pup." The pups live off the decaying "mother" plant until they are big enough to grow on their own.

Last night for dinner, the bromeliad depended on...

A frog lives in this bromeliad.

24

A Famous Bromeliad

Bromeliad may be a new word to many readers. But you've probably nibbled on the most famous bromeliad—the pineapple. Christopher Columbus first brought pineapples from the New World to Europe in 1494. Pineapples were a huge hit in Europe—people loved the naturally sweet food.

Soon this simple jungle bromeliad became popular with kings, queens, and wealthy people. Pineapples were so rare and so delicious that they were served at important dinners. Over time, pineapples became more common in Europe and colonial America. More people could afford to serve them at special meals. Pineapples then became a symbol of good hospitality—welcoming guests to a home.

... fungus and other decomposers. To find out what the fungus and other decomposers are up to, TURN TO PAGE 32.

... lianas. Lianas also lend support to the bromeliads. To find out what the lianas, vines, and creepers of the rain forest are like, TURN TO PAGE 50.

... trees. Without the trees, most bromeliads would never survive. To find out what the trees of the rain forest are like, TURN TO PAGE 43.

ANACONDA *(Eunectes murinus)*

The anaconda swishes through the shallow, murky river water. Only her eyes and nose are visible. Behind her, the water hides her enormous body. She's 20 feet (6 meters) long. Anacondas aren't the longest snakes in the world, but they are the heaviest. They can easily weigh 300 pounds (136 kilograms) and be as thick as an adult human. This big, heavy snake moves fastest when she's in the water.

The sun rises higher in the sky. The anaconda heads for shore. She drapes herself in the brush along the shore now. She needs to soak up the warmth of the sun to raise her body temperature.

Nearby, an alligator suns himself as well. He's a smaller one— only 3 feet (1 meter) long—and no match for the anaconda. In a

Baby Anacondas

When anacondas mate, a female and up to twelve males twist and knot together in what scientists call a breeding ball. It's a slow-motion fight for the males to be the one to mate with her. They'll stay tangled up for two to four weeks!

Baby anacondas are born live and up to one hundred at a time. The birds and lizards of the jungle snap up most of the babies right away as food. But a few will live long enough to grow to the gigantic adult size.

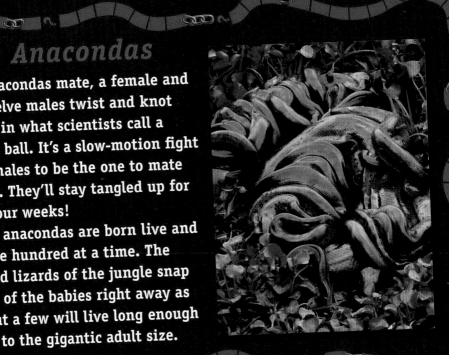

flash, she shoots across the space between them. She sinks her one hundred teeth into the alligator's tough hide to hold him steady. Then she wraps her length around him. Around and around and around again. The pressure is so tight that the alligator can't breathe. In minutes he is dead. Now she's ready to gulp him down whole.

The anaconda unwinds herself. At first, it seems there's no way the alligator can fit inside her. But anacondas come prepared. Her lower jaw is split in the middle, and she has a special muscle that connects her upper and lower jaw. This allows her to unhinge her jaw—so that even enormous meals can fit through.

She starts at the head of the alligator. His legs will fold against his body—and not poke her insides—as he goes down. Her throat muscles ripple, crushing him and dragging his body in further. She breathes through a windpipe at the bottom of her mouth. It's a slow, slow process. She swallows him inch by inch. She has to get the alligator down before his body starts to **decompose**. If she's stuck with a half-swallowed, rotting meal in her mouth, she could die.

Inside her, powerful chemicals kick in to digest the alligator. Anacondas can't break down hair and teeth. But they can dissolve other tough stuff, such as bones and beaks. It just takes time. The anaconda will have a lumpy middle for weeks to come. This meal will last her for months and months.

Last year *for dinner, the anaconda swallowed . . .*

. . . a black howler monkey dozing on a branch. To find out what another black howler monkey is up to, TURN TO PAGE 34.

. . . a capybara swimming in the river. To find out what another capybara is up to, TURN TO PAGE 12.

. . . a golden lion tamarin eating a piece of fruit. To find out what another golden lion tamarin is up to, TURN TO PAGE 46.

. . . a two-toed sloth climbing up a tree. To find out what another two-toed sloth is up to, TURN TO PAGE 14.

. . . a green iguana basking in the sun. To find out what another green iguana is up to, TURN TO PAGE 18.

. . . a hoatzin flapping near the ground. To find out what another hoatzin is up to, TURN TO PAGE 56.

. . . a young giant anteater licking up ants. To find out what another giant anteater is up to, TURN TO PAGE 22.

GIANT ARMADILLO *(Priodontes maximus)*

Uh, oh. **DEAD END!** The giant armadillo has existed for at least two million years. But the species is **endangered**, and this armadillo is pretty lonely in the jungle.

She's covered by supersized armor. It's made of bone, and it covers everything except her belly and the tip of her nose. The armor puts off many predators, which can't bite or claw through it. But her armor doesn't protect her from human dangers. Humans have destroyed parts of the armadillos' habitat. They've also overhunted the animals.

Farmers often kill armadillos because they think the digging ruins crops. But armadillos may actually help farmers. Giant armadillos play an important part in keeping the leaf-cutter ant population under control. Without giant armadillos, leaf-cutter ants would chew away at the farmers' plants.

Armadillos and Medicine

Armadillos are the only other animal besides humans that can get leprosy, a disease of the skin. Scientists can use armadillos to learn more about the disease and how to cure it in humans. Many other rain forest animals and plants may be able to help humans. But the destruction of the rain forest is happening so quickly that many species are destroyed before scientists can study them. Are we cutting down a cure for cancer?

LEAF-CUTTER ANTS *(Atta cephalotes)*

What's *that*? Tiny leaves marching down the trunk of the tree? Well, take a step closer. Now you'll see that under each bit of leaf is an ant. These are leaf-cutter ants. To be even more exact—they are the media leaf-cutter ants. Thousands of them trek up the giant trunk and out along the wide branches. They nip a chunk of a leaf bigger than their own bodies. Then they balance it like a sail over their heads as they haul it all the way back down to the nest beneath the forest floor. It would be as if you were walking miles and miles for lunch.

At the nest, their coworkers, the minima leaf-cutter ants, take over. They take the leaves deep underground. There they chew them up and then mix the pulp with poop. Out of the mix grows a special fungus. The fungus is the ants' only food, and without the leaves, it won't grow.

The ant queen lives in the underground nest. She started the **colony**, and she lays all the eggs. The colony may grow to more than five million ants. A colony with that many leaf-cutter ants can pluck a tree bare in just a few hours—one piece of a leaf at a time.

Last night for dinner, the ants cut leaves from...

Guard Ants

Leaf-cutter ant colonies also include guard ants. They watch out for any danger—such as parasitic wasps. Parasitic wasps don't buzz and sting like the ones you may be familiar with. Instead, they use their stinger to lay eggs inside the heads of the worker ants. A guard ant will often hitch a ride on a leaf being carried by a media ant. The guard protects the media ant as it does its work.

... bromeliads. To find out what the bromeliads of the rain forest are like, TURN TO PAGE 24.

... woody vines and lianas. To find out what the lianas, vines, and creepers of the rain forest are like, TURN TO PAGE 50.

... a cacao tree. To find out what the trees of the rain forest are like, TURN TO PAGE 43.

FUNGUS AND OTHER DECOMPOSERS

Life on the floor of the rain forest changes very quickly. In a northern forest, dead animals might take months to **decompose**. But in a rain forest, the carcasses of those dead animals will be completely reabsorbed by the jungle within six weeks.

The jungle's heat and humidity helps break down dead animals and plants. But the forest floor is also packed with a huge variety of decomposers—fungus, mushrooms, worms, insects, and others. Those decomposers quickly break down animal droppings, dead leaves, fallen branches, and carcasses. They recycle it all back into the soil as nutrients. The rain forest plants use those nutrients as food. It's a good thing too, because the soil of the rain forest doesn't provide many nutrients on its own.

Last night for dinner, the decomposers got to work on...

Top: Mushrooms
Bottom: Bird's-nest fungus

. . . the carcass of a jaguar. To find out what another jaguar is up to, TURN TO PAGE 8.

. . . the carcass of a giant armadillo. To find out what another giant armadillo is up to, TURN TO PAGE 29.

. . . the carcass of a giant anteater. To find out what another giant anteater is up to, TURN TO PAGE 22.

. . . the carcass of a harpy eagle. To find out what another harpy eagle is up to, TURN TO PAGE 37.

. . . a fallen bromeliad flower. To find out what the bromeliads of the rain forest are like, TURN TO PAGE 24.

. . . the nuts from a cacao tree. To find out what the trees of the rain forest are like, TURN TO PAGE 43.

. . . the carcass of an anaconda. To find out what another anaconda is up to, TURN TO PAGE 26.

. . . the remains of army ants. To find out what other army ants are up to, TURN TO PAGE 58.

BLACK HOWLER MONKEY (Alouatta caraya)

Rawhr—awhr—reech! The monkey's call echoes through the jungle. It joins the calls from the seven members of her troop (the group she lives with). The noise—a mix of a grunt, a croak, and a screech—is incredibly loud. Howlers have an extralarge jaw, neck, and vocal cords for this. In fact, howler monkeys are the loudest creatures in the New World. They're even louder than your little brother or sister! They can be heard up to 3 miles (5 kilometers) away. If any other howler monkeys are in the area, they'll answer the call.

Howler monkeys rest almost nineteen hours a day. But this troop is on the move. They're looking for fresh new leaves to feed on. Most monkeys eat some meat or insects, but not howlers. They're strictly vegetarian.

They swing from branch to branch, using their **prehensile** tails like third arms. The tails are hairless underneath so that the monkeys can feel and grip better.

Monkey Talk

Howlers howl because they're defending their neighborhood. They usually live and roam within an area about the size of a large school playground, and they'll fight to defend their space. Each morning and evening, they check in with other troops by howling. People have found out that when howlers don't have neighbors—such as in a zoo—they don't howl nearly as much. So zookeepers play recordings of monkeys howling in the distance. The zoo troop answers—and feels right at home.

The females in a troop are easy to pick out. They're smaller than males, with brown fur, not black. The females share the responsibility of raising the youngest members of their troop. Sometimes males help too, but not the youngest males. Young males sometimes kill the babies.

With a few more calls, the troop settles in among treetops and starts munching. *Last night for dinner, they dined on...*

...leaves from a strangler fig. To find out what the lianas, vines, and creepers of the rain forest are like, TURN TO PAGE 50.

...leaves from a bromeliad. To find out what the bromeliads of the rain forest are like, TURN TO PAGE 24.

...leaves from a cannonball tree. To find out what the trees of the rain forest are like, TURN TO PAGE 43.

HARPY EAGLE *(Harpia harpyja)*

The harpy eagle perches near the top branch of a kapok tree. She's been parked here for more than four hours—but she's not necessarily resting. North American eagles soar over their hunting areas looking for food. But harpy eagles prefer to watch and listen when they hunt. And she's excellent at it. Her dishlike face is designed to help capture sounds, and she can spy a tiny butterfly from more than 600 feet (183 meters) away.

Finally, she sees what she's been looking for. She spreads her long, powerful wings and swoops down. She pours on the speed, reaching 50 miles (80 kilometers) per hour—almost highway speed to us. As she nears the ground, she spreads her ferocious talons (claws) and steals a monkey from his group. Her talons, bigger than a bear's claws, crush the monkey's head. The monkey is killed instantly.

The monkey's body is heavy. She takes a break on a nearby branch to gobble down pieces of him. Once she's lightened her load, she heads back to the kapok.

She flaps up. She can fly nearly straight up—something that comes in handy in the dense forest. At almost twenty stories high, her kapok is the tallest tree around. The tree has broken through the **canopy** and towers over the rest of the rain forest. Waiting for her in her nest at the top is her fledgling and her mate.

Harpy eagles have a huge wingspan (the measurement from the tip of one outspread wing to the tip of the other). Their wingspans average 6.5 feet (2 m).

The stick nest she lands in has plenty of room for the three of them. There's enough space so that even you could stretch out in it. She and her mate rip strips of flesh off their **prey** and feed them to their two-month-old chick.

As with most newborns, he's been their whole life for months. Harpy eagles only have offspring every two to three years. This eagle laid two eggs four months ago. She and her mate kept them warm for two months. But when the first egg hatched, the second was left to die. Since then the harpy eagle and her mate take turns feeding the single chick.

The male eagle is much smaller than the female, so he hunts for smaller prey. He tends to catch rodents and lizards, while she goes for bigger animals. By teaming up, they make sure their family gets a wide variety of food.

Last night for dinner, the family feasted on...

Harpies

Harpy eagles are named after harpies in Greek mythology. In myths, harpies were spirits with the bodies of eagles and the faces of women. They carried the dead to Hades, the land of the dead. Artists also studied the harpy eagle—with its owl-like face and tufted head—when they designed the mythical phoenix in the Harry Potter movies.

. . . **a capybara just on the edge of her group.** To find out what another capybara is up to, TURN TO PAGE 12.

. . . **a black howler monkey resting in the canopy.** To find out what another black howler monkey is up to, TURN TO PAGE 34.

. . . **a two-toed sloth that couldn't get away in time.** To find out what another two-toed sloth is up to, TURN TO PAGE 14.

. . . **a golden lion tamarin calling for a mate.** To find out what another golden lion tamarin is up to, TURN TO PAGE 46.

. . . **an eyelash viper stretched out on a twig.** To find out what another eyelash viper is up to, TURN TO PAGE 48.

. . . **a newborn anaconda twined around a tree.** To find out what another anaconda is up to, TURN TO PAGE 26.

. . . **a baby giant armadillo crossing a clearing in the forest.** To find out what another giant armadillo is up to, TURN TO PAGE 29.

SWALLOW-TAILED HUMMINGBIRD

(Eupetomena macroura)

Zip! A swallow-tailed hummingbird zings by. He stops to take a sip of nectar (a sweet liquid that flowers make) from a pink bromeliad. Inside his long, narrow beak is a long, narrow tongue. With it, he laps up the tasty nectar.

While he drinks, he hovers in one place, like a helicopter. His wings "hum" in a rapid figure-eight pattern

The swallow-tailed hummingbird is one of the world's largest hummingbirds. It can grow to be about 6 inches (15 centimeters) long from the tip of its beak to the tip of its tail.

that keeps him in the air. Hummingbirds are the only birds that can do this. They can also fly sideways and backward. When other birds are flying, they need to move forward constantly or they'll fall.

The flower nectar that hummingbirds love so much is almost all sugar. The birds need a lot of sugar—almost half their weight a day—to survive. So they flit from flower to flower. As they go, they pick up pollen from one flower and carry it to the next. Pollen is a powder that flowers use to make seeds. The flowers will drop their seeds on the ground, and the seeds will sprout new flowers. So by **pollinating**, hummingbirds help flowers thrive and spread.

Uh oh! The hummingbird catches sight of another nearby. A high-speed pursuit begins as the hummingbird chases off the intruder. Hummingbirds are not very friendly. They don't like to share—even with their own kind.

Last night for dinner, this hummingbird visited . . .

Bird-Friendly Coffee

Did you know there's hummingbird-safe coffee? The Smithsonian Migratory Bird Center at the National Zoo in Washington, D.C., promotes bird-friendly coffee. Coffee beans are a natural rain forest product. But many coffee growers cut down all the trees on their plantations (large farms). They can grow more coffee crops on the cleared land. But cutting down trees kills off birds, including hummingbirds. Certified bird-friendly coffee is grown in shade—at plantations that have kept their trees.

. . . liana flowers. To find out what the lianas, vines, and creepers of the rain forest are like, TURN TO PAGE 50.

. . . bromeliad flowers. To find out what the bromeliads of the rain forest are like, TURN TO PAGE 24.

. . . the flowers of a tree. To find out what the trees of the rain forest are like, TURN TO PAGE 43.

TERMITES *(Isoptera)*

The termites crawl in and out, over and under the crumbling log. Many people compare termites to ants, because they also live in **colonies** and look similar to ants. But if you look closely, termites have shorter legs and are fatter and slower than ants.

In fact, termites aren't related to ants at all. They are most closely related to cockroaches. Like cockroaches, they are **detritivores**. Termites' jaws are like tiny saws. They cut off bits of fallen tree branches. The termites are after the fibers inside the wood. But by cutting up the wood, they help to break down and recycle the forest so new plants can grow.

The bits of wood are taken back to the colony. Many termite colonies are made up of complicated nests and tunnels. They contain dirt, chewed-up wood, spit, and poop. Sometimes these nests are so strong that even bulldozers can't break them apart.

Termites don't attack living wood, so trees in the rain forest are safe. But when termites live near people, they can be a huge nuisance. Termites can badly damage homes and buildings by attacking the wood inside the walls.

Last night (and every night) for dinner, termites munched on...

42

Termite Energy

Scientist Steven Chu thinks that we might be able to learn how to create pollution-free energy from termites. Termites have bacteria in their guts that turn cellulose into ethanol. Ethanol is a fuel we already use. It's created from corn. But using corn for fuel means there's less corn for people to eat. If we can figure out how the termites do it, then perhaps we, too, can create a fuel that won't pollute the environment and won't use up food crops.

...wood, wood, and more wood. Good thing there are all those trees! To find out what the trees of the rain forest are like, TURN TO PAGE 43.

TREES OF THE RAIN FOREST

Rain forest trees are the "green treasures" of the jungle. In just 1 acre (0.4 hectare) of rain forest, you can find almost one hundred different species of trees. In a northern forest, you would usually find only ten species

The rain forest's thick **canopy** layer is crammed with huge leaves. Each leaf is trying to be bigger that the next and gather more sunlight. Above the canopy is the emergent layer. It's made up of tall trees that poke up through the canopy.

All the creatures of the rain forest depend on the trees for their survival. The thick leaves of the rain forest actually trap rainfall and release the moisture back into the forest. The released moisture travels upward and creates rain clouds. The rain cycle begins again. But when the trees are cut down, all that moisture is lost and the land becomes dry.

water

oxygen

carbon dioxide

Plants make food and oxygen through photosynthesis. Photosynthesis uses sunlight, carbon dioxide (a gas found in air and water), and water. The plants draw in carbon dioxide and water. Then they use the energy from sunlight to turn the carbon dioxide and water into their food.

Rain forest trees also remove lots of harmful carbon dioxide from the air and replace it with oxygen. All living things need oxygen— including humans. Yet people continue to cut down rain forests. They often cut down the trees to make room for farmland. But rain forest soil is not good for growing crops. So farmers have to clear even more land to make money.

We are learning more and more about how the loss of rain forest trees affects animals, other plants, and people. The loss of rain forests is happening rapidly. Many environmentalists (people who work to protect natural habitats) think we should stop clearing land before it is too late.

In the meantime, the rain forest trees continue to take their food from the sun and soil. *Last night for dinner, the trees soaked up nutrients left behind from . . .*

Yummy Trees

Did you know that your chocolate bar may be from the rain forest? The cacao tree grows huge pods full of seeds. The seeds are cocoa beans and are the key ingredients in good-quality chocolate. The brazil nut tree also produces a tasty treat. But watch out for the nuts while you're in the forest! Brazil nuts can weigh up to 5 pounds (2.3 kilograms). When the heavy nuts drop from the trees, they can hit the ground at more than 50 miles (80 kilometers) per hour. The nuts break open, and they are full of edible seeds.

... rhinoceros beetle larvas.
To find out what another rhinoceros beetle is up to, TURN TO PAGE 52.

... fungus and other decomposers. To find out what the fungus and other decomposers of the rain forest are like, TURN TO PAGE 32.

GOLDEN LION TAMARIN *(Leontopithecus rosalia)*

Sorry, **DEAD END.** The golden lion tamarin is hard to find these days in the rain forest. Not that long ago, these monkeys with wild orange manes and blue eyes were swinging through the trees. Now the forests the tamarins called home have been divided up and cleared of trees. The land is being used for farming, and the trees are used for lumber and charcoal.

The golden lion tamarins have been doing better recently. A few decades ago, researchers counted only about 400 living in the wild. In the 2000s, researchers estimate that there are about 1,500 in the wild. But the species is still struggling.

They live in the lower parts of the trees and need old forest growth to survive. The thick trunks, brush, and vines of an old forest take a long time to regrow—if they are allowed to grow back. This tamarin has been released into the wild after being born in a zoo. A lot of people are hoping she'll thrive in her new habitat and start a new family.

New World Monkeys

Only New World monkeys have prehensile tails. Monkeys in Africa and Asia can't use their tails as the golden lion tamarin does. The tamarin often hangs by its tail to reach more fruit. New World monkeys also have thirty-six teeth instead of thirty-two, and they have wider noses than Old World monkeys.

A RAIN FOREST FOOD WEB

Energy moves around the food chain from the sun to plants, from plants to plant eaters, and from animals to the creatures that eat them. Energy also moves from dead animals to the plants and animals that draw nutrients from them.

EYELASH VIPER *(Bothriechis schlegelii)*

The viper tucks himself along the branch. He's almost impossible to spot. Eyelash vipers can be brown, green, reddish yellow, or yellow—to match the flowers they like to hide near. They get their name from the raised scales above their eyes, which look like eyelashes. Like their coloring, the pattern of the scales helps them look like a vine on the branch.

He waits, hoping that a small animal will venture by. Then watch out! He'll spring into action, sinking his deadly fangs into the animal. His fangs shoot venom, or poison, into his **prey**.

He particularly likes birds. The fact that they can fly away isn't a problem for him. His tail is **prehensile**. That means he can twist it around a branch and use it to support the rest of his body. If a bird stops at one of the flowers for a drink of nectar, he can push himself up and snatch it in midair.

His venom kills within minutes. It attacks his prey's central nervous system (the brain, spine, and nerves). Soon the prey will be unable to move or even breathe. Then the viper will swallow it.

Last night for dinner, the viper grabbed . . .

. . . **a green iguana, sunning himself.** To find out what another green iguana is up to, TURN TO PAGE 18.

. . . **an antbird, waiting for some leftovers.** To find out what another antbird is up to, TURN TO PAGE 18.

. . . **a swallow-tailed hummingbird.** Even they are not too quick for a viper. To find out what another swallow-tailed hummingbird is up to, TURN TO PAGE 40.

. . . **a giant monkey frog, resting in a bromeliad.** To find out what another giant monkey frog is up to, TURN TO PAGE 54.

. . . **a baby hoatzin, clinging to a branch.** To find out what another hoatzin is up to, TURN TO PAGE 58.

LIANAS, VINES, AND CREEPERS

High above a forest floor is the **canopy**—the layer where the treetops meet. The rain forest canopy is knitted with vines, creepers (plants that cling to a surface), and lianas (woody vines). They twist, climb, curl, and hang as they compete with the trees for the sunlight. The rain forest has more than 2,500 species. They range from threadlike vines to thick lianas you'd mistake for a tree.

Most lianas, vines, and creepers start life as shrub that leans against a tree. Then sometimes the shrub snakes a tendril or two up the side of the trunk. Others grow on their own. There's actually an amazing variety of ways these plants attach themselves. Clasping tendrils, adhesive hairs, thorns, and suckers—all are used in the plants' upward journey to find sunlight.

Last night for dinner, the lianas and vines soaked up nutrients left behind from . . .

Guaraná

A vinelike shrub called guaraná produces small red orange fruit. For centuries, native people picked the fruit and used its seeds to make a popular drink. The black seeds contain four to five times more caffeine than coffee. Brazilians harvest guaraná seeds to make carbonated soft drinks and energy drinks packaged by companies such as Coca-Cola.

Strangler Figs

In some cases, vines grow from the canopy down. When they reach the soil, then they send out roots. One such plant is the strangler fig. As the strangler fig twines around the tree, it grows sturdy, like a frame around its host tree. At the same time, it leafs out in the canopy. Eventually, it sprouts leaves that shade the host tree like an umbrella. Without the sunlight, the host tree then dies. That leaves the strangler fig standing strong around the hollow core where the tree once was.

... fungus and other decomposers. To find out what the fungus and other decomposers of the rain forest are like, TURN TO PAGE 32.

... a rhinoceros beetle larva. To find out what another rhinoceros beetle is up to, TURN TO PAGE 52.

RHINOCEROS BEETLE *(Oryctes rhinoceros)*

The rhinoceros beetle snuffles through the dead leaves. A rotting stick blocks his way. Without hesitation, the beetle lowers his enormous "horn" and shoves it aside. That was nothing. The rhinoceros beetle is the strongest animal—*in the world*. He can carry up to 850 times his own weight. Imagine a real rhino being able to lift 850 other rhinos. Or imagine that you could lift 850 kids at one time!

The beetle scurries on. He is a decomposer. He's helping to clean up the forest floor by munching on the fallen leaves and fruit. But when he was younger, he really cleaned up. Rhinoceros beetle **larvas** scour the forest floor and gobble up rotting wood. They help to recycle the forest.

Last night for dinner, the beetle scrounged up...

Tons of Insects

The Amazon rain forest has an amazing number of insects. More than thirty million different kinds belonging to thousands of species can be found on just one tree! In fact, if you added up the weight of all the insects, they would weigh more than any other living thing (except the trees themselves) in the jungle.

. . . bromeliad flowers. To find out what the bromeliads of the rain forest are like, TURN TO PAGE 24.

. . . liana leaves. To find out what the lianas, vines, and creepers of the rain forest are like, TURN TO PAGE 50.

. . . fallen rubber tree leaves. To find out what the trees of the rain forest are like, TURN TO PAGE 43.

. . . fungus growing on a tree trunk. To find out what the fungus and other decomposers of the rain forest are like, TURN TO PAGE 32.

GIANT MONKEY FROG *(Phyllomedusa bicolor)*

High up in the canopy, the giant monkey frog clings to a leaf. She'll spend her whole life up here. Frogs in North America are often found in ponds and other bodies of water. But in the rain forests of South America, frogs are mostly found up in the trees. The rain forest air is full of moisture. So the frogs can stay wet without worrying about predators on the ground and in the water.

Instead of webbed feet, the giant monkey frog has separated toes so she can climb better. (Her climbing ability is how she got her name.) She has developed huge eyes too. They help her find all those insects in the dark.

But right now, she's paying attention to something else. From a lower branch comes a clucking sound and then a low note. It's the call of a male monkey frog. She climbs down to meet him. When she finds him, she'll decide if she likes him. If she does, they'll mate. Together they'll find a cone-shaped leaf, such as on a bromeliad plant. Water gathers in the bottom of these leaves, forming a sort of minipond. The minipond provides a perfect environment for the frogs to lay their eggs. Often, generations of tree frogs will enjoy the same miniponds, season after season.

Last night for dinner, the giant monkey frog caught...

Rain Forest Cures

There's a high-tech debate going on about the giant monkey frog. For years, South American native peoples have scraped the poisonous slime off the frogs. They use it in ceremonies and to cure illnesses. Researchers for modern drug companies are very interested in the frog slime. They hope that it can be made into medicine for brain disorders and other medical problems. And frog slime isn't the only medicine in the rain forest. The leaves of rain forest plants could also lead to cures and treatments.

The research seems promising. But the government of Brazil has stepped in. The government knows that the drug companies could make millions of dollars on new medicines. Brazil wants the companies to share that money with the native people of the rain forest.

... a rhinoceros beetle munching through a rotten log. To find out what another rhinoceros beetle is up to, TURN TO PAGE 52.

... a newborn eyelash viper. To find out what another eyelash viper is up to, TURN TO PAGE 48.

... a couple of termites on a lower branch. To find out what other termites are up to, TURN TO PAGE 42.

... a whole row of leaf-cutter ants. To find out what other leaf-cutter ants are up to, TURN TO PAGE 30.

... a pink-toed tarantula, hidden under a leaf. To find out what another pink-toed tarantula is up to, TURN TO PAGE 20.

HOATZIN *(Opisthocomus hoazin)*

The hoatzin chick stretches out its scrawny, almost featherless neck. He's hoping that his mother will cough up some warm cud, or food that she's already chewed. But he's getting too big to be fed. His mother pulls away.

He crawls out of the nest, clinging to the bark of the tree with claws at the top fold of his wings. Those claws will disappear as he grows feathers and gets bigger. For now, he creeps up to where other hoatzins roost. He looks around for some leaves to eat.

Phew! He doesn't notice it because he's used to it, but hoatzins smell! They like swamp plants, such as arum, which are hard to digest. The birds break down the leaves by letting them ferment, or rot, in their guts. The rotting vegetation makes the birds especially stinky. Most predators have to be really hungry before they'll eat a hoatzin.

Suddenly, a screech echoes through the jungle. Some older birds stretch their wings wide, showing their chest. A hoatzin's chest has a large black spot with a white circle around it. The marking looks like a big eye and scares many predators away. Some of the other birds scatter—or try to. They coast clumsily to branches on a different tree.

The baby hoatzin has his own instincts. He releases his claws and tumbles over—splash!—right into a small pond below. Just in time. The monkey who was hoping for a snack peers down at him from the branch above. The monkey soon leaves to find food elsewhere. Then the hoatzin will have a long crawl back up to his roost.

Last night for dinner, the hoatzin crunched...

Where Do Hoatzins Fit?

For years, scientists argued about what type of bird the hoatzin is. What other bird species are they related to? Their clawed wings reminded many scientists of a prehistoric dinosaur bird, *Archaeopteryx*. Others thought the hoatzin was related to more modern birds, such as pheasants, chickens, or turkeys. After years of debate, scientists think that the hoatzin's closest relative is the cuckoo.

. . . leaves from a vine. To find out what the lianas, vines, and creepers of the rain forest are like, TURN TO PAGE 50.

. . . leaves from a bromeliad. To find out what the bromeliads of the rain forest are like, TURN TO PAGE 24.

. . . leaves from a kapok tree. To find out what the trees of the rain forest are like, TURN TO PAGE 43.

ARMY ANTS *(Eciton burchelli)*

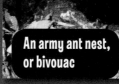

An army ant nest, or bivouac

Beware! An army of half a million is marching across the jungle floor. Don't let their small size fool you. As they come near, the ground begins to squirm. All the living things leap, hop, scamper, and fly to get out of the way. They know that this army will devour everything in its path.

This swarm of army ants is as wide as your bedroom and almost as long as a football field. Right now, they are in their nomadic mode. That means they don't have a permanent nest that they call home. Instead, each day they set out across the jungle floor in search of new food and a new place to sleep at night.

The ants at the front of the swarm strike and kill their **prey**. They sink their large jaws, called mandibles, into whatever they come across. They don't stop to deal with their mess. The ants behind them will take over. They cut up the kill and carry it back to the center of the swarm.

But look out! On the outside edge of the swarm, a lizard flicks his tongue, watching. He's not the only one watching. Some animals follow the ants, hoping for some of the free food the ants stir up on the jungle floor. Some animals might even try to snatch a few ants as well.

But before the lizard can even think to swipe a few ants, a guard ant nips it with its enormous mandibles. Wisely, the lizard clears out before it, too, becomes food for the swarm.

More and more ants are headed to the center of the swarm. Despite being blind, they never run into one another. The first ants leave a trail. The ants behind them follow it, and soon traffic lanes appear. In fact, ants do this so well that humans have studied their "rules" to see if there is anything we can use to solve our own traffic problems. Using these lanes, the ants catch and kill more than thirty thousand creatures in their raid.

But now, it's time to rest. The workers hook their legs together and form a living nest, called a bivouac. Inside, all their hard-won food is sucked down.

In their nomadic phase, army ants will move and hunt every day. *Last night for dinner, they slurped...*

Ant Stitches

Have you ever gotten stitches for a big cut? The stitches hold the cut together so it can heal. Native South Americans sometimes use army ants for the same thing. They press the huge mandibles of a guard ant against a cut. The ant bites around the wound and pulls the edges together. Then they twist the ant's body off. The mandibles remain, closing the cut so that it will stop bleeding and heal.

. . . a rhinoceros beetle, surprised by the ant stampede. To find out what another rhinoceros beetle is up to, TURN TO PAGE 52.

. . . a baby antbird, fallen from its nest. To find out what another antbird is up to, TURN TO PAGE 16.

. . . a pink-toed tarantula, caught in the swarm of ants. To find out what another pink-toed tarantula is up to, TURN TO PAGE 20.

. . . a young green iguana that didn't scurry away fast enough. To find out what another green iguana is up to, TURN TO PAGE 18.

GLOSSARY

bacteria: tiny living things made up of only one cell

canopy: the highest branchy layer of a forest formed by the treetops

carnivore: an animal that eats other animals

colony: a mass of plants or animals of one species that live together

decompose: to decay, or break down, after dying

decomposers: living things, such as insects or bacteria, that feed on dead plants and animals

detritivores: creatures that use plant and animal waste as food

endangered: close to dying out

epiphytes: plants that grow on other plants but get water and nutrients from the air and rain

food chain: a system in which energy is transferred from plants to animals as each eats and is eaten

food web: many food chains linked together

habitats: areas where a particular group of plants or animals naturally lives and grows

larva: the wormlike stage in an insect's life between the egg and adult forms

New World: the landmass of North America, Central America, and South America

nutrients: substances, especially in food, that help a plant or animal survive

pollinate: to carry a flower's seed-making material from one plant to another

predators: animals that hunt and kill other animals for food

prehensile: able to grasp and hold onto things

prey: animals that are hunted for food by other animals

primary consumers: animals that eat plants

producers: living things that make their own food

rain forest: a thick forest that normally gets more than 160 inches (406 centimeters) of rain a year

secondary consumers: animals and insects that eat other animals and insects

species: a group of related animals or plants

tertiary consumers: animals that hunt other animals and have few natural enemies

FURTHER READING AND WEBSITES

BOOKS

Forsyth, Adrian. *How Monkeys Make Chocolate: Unlocking the Mysteries of the Rain Forest*. Toronto: Maple Tree Press, 2006. Discover where chocolate, cola, aspirin, and rubber come from and explore what else might be discovered in rain forests.

Goodman, Susan. *Ultimate Field Trip #1: Adventures in the Amazon Rain Forest*. New York: Aladdin, 1999. Seventh- and eighth-grade students travel to the Amazon to learn about the rain forest in this true story.

Markle, Sandra. *Army Ants*. Minneapolis: Lerner Publications Company, 2005. This book in the Animal Scavengers series takes a detailed look at the rain forest's own cleanup crew.

Stewart, Melissa. *New World Monkeys*. Minneapolis: Lerner Publications Company, 2008. This Nature Watch book looks at the many species of monkeys living in the rain forests of Central and South America.

Walker, Sally. *Jaguars*. Minneapolis: Lerner Publications Company, 2009. Walker details the life and habits of the New World's strongest predator.

Welsbacher, Anne. *Protecting the Earth's Rain Forests*. Minneapolis: Lerner Publications Company, 2009. Part of the Saving Our Living Earth series, this book looks at the problems facing the world's rain forests and how we can help.

WEBSITES

Amazonia
http://nationalzoo.si.edu/Animals/Amazonia
Learn all about the Amazon exhibits at the National Zoo in Washington, D.C.

Amazon Interactive
http://www.eduweb.com/amazon.html
Learn about the Amazon, and then try your hand at creating an ecotourism business.

Amazon: Sights and Sounds
http://www.worldwildlife.org/wildplaces/amazon/sounds.cfm
Hear the jaguar's growl and the macaw's call on these pages.

Journey into Amazonia
http://www.pbs.org/journeyintoamazonia
Learn about the PBS series and the jungle and then play Amazon Explorer.

Virtual Amazon Tour
http://www.msu.edu/%7Ecarusosa/rainforest.htm
Take a peek at the rain forest in this Michigan State University site.

SELECTED BIBLIOGRAPHY

Burnie, David, and Don E. Wilson. *Animal: The Definitive Visual Guide to the World's Wildlife*. London: DK, 2005.

Davis, Wade. *River: Explorations and Discoveries in the Amazon Rain Forest*. New York: Simon & Schuster, 1996.

The Encyclopedia of Animals: A Complete Visual Guide. Berkeley: University of California Press, 2004.

Goulding, Michael. *The Smithsonian Atlas of the Amazon*. Washington, DC: Smithsonian Institution Press, 2003.

Hecht, Susanna B. *The Fate of the Forest: Developers, Destroyers, and Defenders of the Amazon*. London: Verso, 1989.

IUCN Species Survival Commission. *2007 IUCN Red List of Threatened Species*. N.d. http://www.iucnredlist.org/ (July 22, 2008).

Rainforest Action Network. "South America." Rainforestweb.org. 2001. http://www.rainforestweb.org/Rainforest_Regions/South_America/ (July 22, 2008).

UNEP-WCMC. "World Conservation Monitoring Centre." *United Nations Environment Programme*. N.d. http://www.unep-wcmc.org/ (July 22, 2008).

University of Michigan Museum of Zoology. *Animal Diversity Web*. 1995–2008. http://animaldiversity.ummz.umich.edu/site/index.html (July 22, 2008).

Whitemore, T. C. *An Introduction to Tropical Rain Forests*. New York: Oxford University Press, 1998.

INDEX

Photo Acknowledgments

The images in this book are used with the permission of: © Stephen Alvarez/
National Geographic/Getty Images, background photographs on pp. 1, 11,
13, 15, 17, 19, 21, 23, 25, 28, 31, 33, 36, 39, 41, 45, 49, 51, 53, 55, 57, 59;
© Mauricio Simonetti/The Image Bank/Getty Images, pp. 4-5, 6-7; © Wendy
Shattil/Stock Connection/drr.net, p. 8; © Tom & Pat Leeson/drr.net, pp. 9, 46;
© James Balog/Digital Vision/Getty Images, p. 10; © Pete Oxford/naturepl.com,
p. 12; © Pete Oxford/Minden Pictures/Getty Images, pp. 14, 35, 56; © Woodfall/
Photoshot/drr.net, p. 16; © Zina Seletskaya -Fotolia.com , p. 18; © Dr Morley
Read/Photo Researchers, Inc., p. 20; © Theo Allofs/Photonica/Getty Images,
p. 22; © Tui De Roy/Minden Pictures/Getty Images, pp. 24 (top), 38; © Paul A.
Zahl/National Geographic/Getty Images, p. 24 (bottom); © Ed George/National
Geographic/Getty Images, p. 26 (top); © Fracois Savigny/naturepl.com, p. 26
(bottom); © Suzi Eszterhas/Minden Pictures/Getty Images, p. 27; © Gabriel
Rojo/naturepl.com, p. 29; © Ken Lucas/Visuals Unlimited, p. 30; © Mark
Moffett/Minden Pictures/Getty Images, p. 32; © Michael & Patricia Fogden/
Minden Pictures/Getty Images, pp. 32 (bottom), 45 (top), 50; © Joel Sartore/
National Geographic/Getty Images, p. 37 (top); © Pete Oxford/DRK PHOTO, p. 37
(bottom); © Genevieve Vallee/Alamy, p. 40; © Peter Essick/Aurora/Getty Images,
p. 42; © Travel Ink/Gallo Images/Getty Images, p. 43 (top); © Cyril Ruoso/JH
Editorial/Minden Pictures/Getty Images, p. 44; © Michael Fogden/DRK PHOTO,
p. 48; © Altrendo Nature/Getty Images, p. 52; © David Delimont/Alamy, p. 54;
© Martin Dohrn/naturepl.com, p. 58. Illustrations for game board and pieces
© Bill Hauser/Independent Picture Service.

Front Cover: © Stephen Alvarez/National Geographic/Getty Images
(background); © Pete Oxford/Minden Pictures/Getty Images (left); © Nat
Photos/Digital Vision/Getty Images (second from left); © James Balog/Digital
Vision/Getty Images (second from right); © SA Team/Foto Natura/Minden
Pictures/Getty Images (right).

About the Authors

Don Wojahn and Becky Wojahn are school library media specialists by day and
writers by night. Their natural habitat is the temperate forests of northwestern
Wisconsin, where they share their den with two animal-loving sons and two
big black dogs. The Wojahns' other Follow that Food Chain books include *A
Temperate Forest Food Chain, A Desert Food Chain, An Australian Outback Food
Chain, A Savanna Food Chain,* and *A Tundra Food Chain.*